THE REAL THING!

SCORPIONS

By Mary Packard

tangerine Press

an imprint of

■SCHOLASTIC

www.scholastic.com

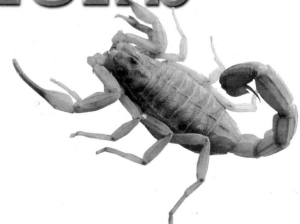

Meet the Scorpions

Arachnids have been on this planet for millions of years and scorpions are no exception. They have been swimming and crawling around for more than 400 million years. Compared to them, we humans are the new kids on the block!

Tityus paraensis male

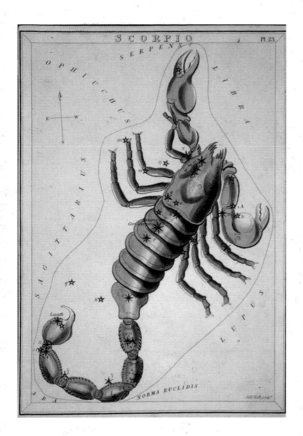

The Babylonians, the first to divide the night sky into constellations, were so impressed with the scorpion's power that they named a constellation Scorpio in their honor.

It's no wonder that so many myths about scorpions have sprung up over the years. Scorpions appear in Greek, Hebrew, and Mayan mythology, among others. The ancient Egyptians, inspired by their belief that scorpions arose from the dead bodies of crocodiles, actually worshipped scorpions as gods.

Serket, the Ancient Egyptian scorpion goddess

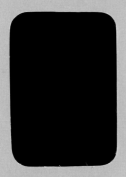

Older Than Dirt

A 325-million-year-old scorpion fossil proves that scorpions made their appearance on Earth even before the dinosaurs! More than 400 million years ago, huge sea scorpions ruled the oceans. These creatures grew to be 3 feet (1 m) long.

This *Archaeobuthus estephani* scorpion was trapped in amber 127 million years ago.

Well fortified against predators, the ancient swimmers had large, bony shells and long tails with broad paddles to help propel them through the water. Over time, as their tails became more pointed, they shed their paddles in favor of bony spikes. When the sea scorpions sprouted legs, they began to resemble the land scorpions we see today.

Fossilized scorpion from the *Protoischnuridae* family,110 million years B.C.E.

Palaeoananteris ribnitiodamgartensis scorpion in amber, 50 million years B.C.E.

When the inland seas and rivers began to dry up, sea scorpions not only survived on land, they also thrived there. Except for their size, scorpions have changed very little over the ages. If you were to see a 400-million-year-old fossil, you'd know what it was right away. The best sea scorpion fossils are found in Upstate New York—which is why its legislature passed a bill in 1984 making the sea scorpion the state fossil.

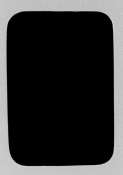

Creature Features

Ranging from $\frac{1}{2}$ in. (1 cm) to 8.5 in. (21 cm) in length, most scorpions are brown, black, or yellowish in color. Scorpions are members of the arachnid class. Arachnids are arthropods. The word *arthropod* means "jointed feet." Like us, arthropods have joints that bend.

You can tell that scorpions are arachnids by counting their legs. Arachnids have eight legs, not six as insects do. And, like other arachnids, scorpions have a two-part body.

The last six segments of a scorpion's abdomen form its tail. It ends in a curved stinger called the telson, and is surrounded by two poison glands that supply the stinger with venom.

The rear section is a long abdomen, or belly, that is divided into segments. The abdomen contains the scorpion's digestive, breathing, and reproductive systems.

Beneath the abdomen are holes called spiracles through which the scorpion breathes.

The short, thick front part, called a cephalothorax, is made up of a fused head and chest.

Attached to the cephalothorax are the legs, chelicerae (jaws), and pedipalps, which in scorpions, have evolved into powerful pincers.

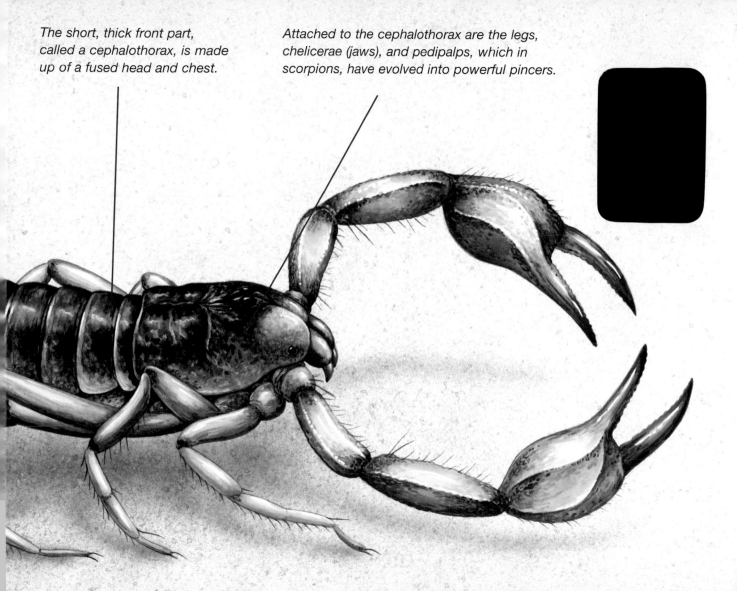

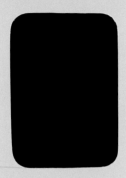

Scorpion Secrets

Creepy, deadly, sneaky— these are words people often use to describe scorpions. In some places, their scary reputation is well deserved. Consider this: In Mexico, more than 1,000 people die from scorpion stings every year, and in Tunisia, a scorpion kills at least one person per day.

Parabuthus mossambicensis

Not all scorpions are deadly, however. Although scientists have identified as many as 1,500 species of scorpions, only 25 are equipped with venom strong enough to kill a person. That such tiny creatures can kill mammals as big as humans with so little effort is pretty awesome.

Scorpions have made themselves at home in every kind of habitat. Some can survive underwater for two days. Others that have been frozen for weeks have returned to normal only a few hours after being thawed out. Scorpions have even been found living near nuclear test sites in Nevada. Apparently, the high level of radiation doesn't bother them! Perhaps that is why those who study scorpions are trying to learn from them. Who knows what other secrets these small arachnids can teach us.

Hadrurus arizonensis

They Want To Be Alone

Burrows take time and energy to construct—and no scorpion is better equipped than the rare giant hairy scorpion. Up to 6 in. (15 cm) long, this scorpion burrows deep into the desert soil, where it dines on lizards.

Scorpio maurus

Israeli gold scorpions are obligate burrowers—which means that if they do not dig themselves a burrow, they will die. Their burrows are up to 27 in. (68 cm) deep, providing them with ample protection from extremes in climate. They can be found in deserts, grasslands, and mountain regions. The pincers of these scorpions are strong enough to move rocks as big as they are. Their venom, however, is too weak to protect them.

Anuroctonus phaiodactylus

The huge pincers of a swollen-stinger scorpion look like dark pointy claws. This two-toned scorpion is also called the dusky-footed scorpion and grows to be about 2.5 in. (6 cm) long. It likes nothing more than to burrow 8 to 12 in. (20 to 30 cm) down into well-packed dirt. Once construction is complete, these shy creatures rarely leave their burrows—not even to hunt! How do they eat? They wait patiently for some tasty critter to drop in.

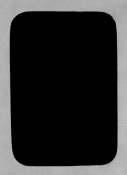

Favorite Hangouts

Wood scorpions live in the forested, rocky areas of Canada and the western United States. To find one, look near creeks, under stones, logs, and dead, decaying leaves. The pincers of this large, menacing-looking predator indicate that its pinch will be more painful than its sting.

Uroctonus mordax

Hadogenes troglodytes

The South African rock scorpion is the longest scorpion in the world. A few have actually reached almost 8 in. (21 cm), but most are between 5 and 7 in. (15 and 20 cm) long. Like other rock-dwelling scorpions, its body is slender and flat, and its tail can bend sideways—good for slipping into cracks and crevices. To further streamline themselves, this slender creature holds its long pincers close to its body, forming a kind of shield to protect itself from the jagged edges of rocks.

Smeringurus mesaensis

Most sand scorpions are yellow to blend in with their surroundings. Sand scorpions have developed a clever trick called stilting. To beat the heat while they're above ground, they stretch tiptoe-like on all eight legs, lifting their bodies off of the hot sand. When it comes to food, these little cannibals prefer their own kind. Vibrations in the sand tell a giant sand scorpion where another scorpion is likely to be. Then it scurries over, digs the unfortunate creature out of its burrow, and eats it.

Scent-sational

Scorpions' pincers are lined with microscopic hairs that are sensitive to vibrations in the air. The vibrations let scorpions know what kind of animals are stirring around them—information that helps them avoid predators and locate their prey.

Male burrowing scorpion

Scorpion pincers

Scorpions also use their pincers to defend themselves and to help them capture, hold, and crush prey. All arachnids have pedipalps, but scorpions are the only animals with a pair of sense organs called pectines. Attached to the bottom front of a scorpion's belly, pectines look like combs lined with 20 to 50 "teeth." Pectines help scorpions find mates by picking up the scent given off by other scorpions of their species.

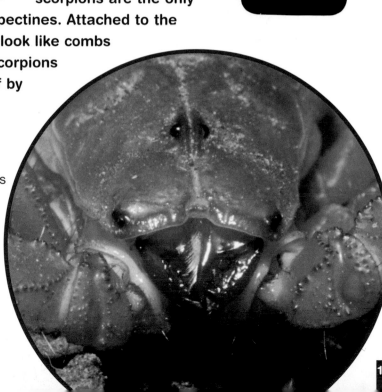

Scorpion eyes

Like most animals that hunt at night, scorpions have poor eyesight, even though they can have up to 12 eyes—a central pair, and two to five smaller eyes on either side of the head. Their eyes work better in low levels of light.

Scorpion Stalkers

Scorpion-hunters travel all over the world to study their subjects. When they hunt at night, they carry portable ultraviolet lights, batteries to power them, long tweezers, gloves, insect repellent, and leggings. The reason for the leggings is that scorpions glow, but snakes do not!

These intrepid scientists climb mountains, tramp through rainforests, put up with sandstorms, and stay up all night just for the chance to discover a new species of scorpion—one that they can name themselves. These scientists are also eager to observe new behaviors in those species that are already known. Scorpion expert Gary Polis, for example, spent five years in the sand dunes of California, where he observed four different species of scorpion. To track the lives of individuals, Polis dotted them with different colors of paint.

Leirus jordanensis,
a new species found in Jordan in 2002

Opisthacanthus

For research purposes, Polis divided each species of scorpion into three categories by age: young—under a year; intermediate—one to two years; and adult—two to six years. The results of his five-year study were startling. There were wider variations in behavior among the different age groups than there were from species to species.

Way To Glow

Scorpions are found almost everywhere on the planet except Antarctica and New Zealand. Most prefer warm regions, although some live in the cool, high Himalayan Mountains of Asia and the Andes Mountains of South America. Scorpions inhabit deserts, forests, and grasslands, as well as caves.

Parabuthus mossambicensis

Newly molted scorpions do not glow, because the substance that causes fluorescence is found only in the hyaline layer of the exoskeleton—a part that forms only as the exoskeleton hardens. The tough hyaline layer is often found in scorpion fossils hundreds of millions of years after the rest of the body has turned to dust!

Orthochirus scrobiculosus

Even though scorpions live almost everywhere, little was known about their habits until recently. Because scorpions hide by day, it was hard for scientists to observe them in their natural habitats. That all changed dramatically when scientists discovered that scorpions fluoresce—a fancy way of saying that when an ultraviolet light is shined around a scorpion's habitat, the scorpion glows in the dark!

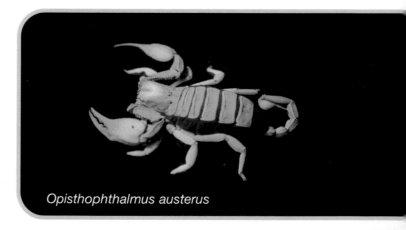

Opisthophthalmus austerus

Couch Potatoes

When it comes to survival, scorpions are superstars. They're also the couch potatoes of the arachnid world. These little carnivores usually wait for their food to come to them—and they're in no hurry. Scorpions can go without eating for more than a year!

Opistachanthus asper

Hadrurus spadix

After they do chow down, scorpions make very economical use of their food. While scorpions get all of the liquids they need through their prey, their efficient, compact bodies continue to recycle it so that very little is lost as bodily waste. What little waste they excrete looks very much like chalk powder.

Amazingly, scorpions have a slower metabolism than some growing vegetables, such as carrots! The least active of all arachnids, scorpions tend not to wear out their parts. In times of drought or famine, they simply shut down until conditions improve. It is probably this quality that accounts for their very long lifespan. Some scorpions live for as long as 25 years—longer than any other arachnid or insect.

Parabuthus stridulus

Parabuthus transvaalicus

What's for Dinner?

One reason that scorpions get along in the world so well is that they will scarf up just about anything that comes their way. When a scorpion is hungry, it waits for nightfall before beginning to hunt.

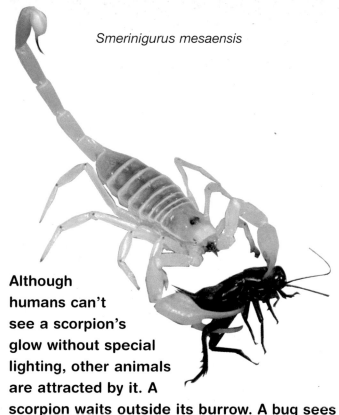

Smerinigurus mesaensis

Although humans can't see a scorpion's glow without special lighting, other animals are attracted by it. A scorpion waits outside its burrow. A bug sees its glow and runs toward the scorpion. When the bug gets close enough—ZAP—it's dinner! Some scorpions eat woodlice, termites, crickets, and beetles. Bigger scorpions are able to catch larger prey, such as lizards, snakes, mice, and birds.

After a scorpion spots its prey, it captures it in its strong pincers. If the prey struggles too much, the scorpion paralyzes it by using its stinger to inject it with venom. Then, the scorpion takes its time, making the meal last for hours. Like other arachnids, a scorpion can't chew, so it turns its food into soup by shooting its prey full of digestive acids from its stomach. The scorpion then sucks up its liquid lunch.

Hadogenes troglodytes

Meercats have no problem catching scorpions

Eat—and Be Eaten

In the animal kingdom, one day you're the predator and the next day you're the prey. Scorpions are snacks for many larger animals, from mice to coyotes—and even other scorpions. Scorpions are one of the few kinds of animals that dine on their own species.

At night, scorpions are scooped up by owls and bats. By day, lizards and snakes hunt scorpions down. Scorpions use their venom to defend themselves. Wary of being stung, an experienced predator will bite off a scorpion's tail before devouring it. Baboons are especially good at this trick!

Scientists have discovered that scorpion venom is a potent mixture of as many as 200 different neurotoxins— poisons that affect the nervous system. Each toxin is effective against a specific kind of prey. One toxin will kill or paralyze mice, while another will work on insects. Yet another kind of poison works on frogs and lizards.

Parabuthus leiosoma

Drop of venom on sting of *Parabuthus transvaalicus*

female

male

Parabuthus transvaalicus couple

Shall We Dance?

Scorpions mate for the first time when they are between two and six years old. When a female is ready to mate, she sends out chemical scents called pheromones into the air. The male picks up the scent through his pectines, and it's not long before he comes crawling.

The male scorpion then leads the female in a courtship dance that scientists call a *promenade à deux*—or a "dance for two." The two scorpions face each other and the male grasps the female's pincers in his own. They move together in this way back and forth, back and forth, covering quite a distance across the ground, sometimes "dancing" for hours.

Scorpion spermatophore

Parabuthus mossambicensis

Eventually they stop and the male scorpion drops a stick-shaped bundle of sperm on the ground. The female receives it through a tiny opening in her abdomen. Because female scorpions are larger than males, mating is a risky business for the male. As soon as the courtship is over, male scorpions hightail it away from their partners—so they don't end up as dinner.

Babies on Board

Scorpion babies do not hatch from eggs, but develop inside their mother—a process that takes from 3 to 18 months. Then when they are ready, a scorpion female gives birth to live babies that are enclosed in a sac, or membrane.

Uroplectes female giving birth

The average number of young in a litter is 30. Because the babies are born one at a time, a female scorpion may spend several days in childbirth. Once the scorplings are born, they wriggle out of their sacs and scramble onto their mother's back. Until their soft, white exoskeleton hardens, babies are totally dependent on their mother. They survive on food that has been stored up in their tiny bodies and drink water that passes through their mother's exoskeleton.

A female scorpion is extremely attentive to her babies. Should one of them slip off her back, she will gently nudge it back into place. Scorpion babies ride around on their mother's back for several weeks. After they molt for the first time, they have a new, darker exoskeleton. When the new skin is hardened, the baby scorpions leap off their mother's back and scatter away. Should they happen to meet their mother again, they are likely to end up as her dinner!

A *Uroplectes* female with newborn scorplings on her back

Heterometrus laoticus

Snug as a Bug

Like all arachnids, scorpions are invertebrates—animals that have no backbone. Instead, a scorpion has an exoskeleton on the outside of its body. This hard exoskeleton is made of a substance called chitin and protects the scorpion's soft insides.

Heterometrus species

The exoskeleton is so rigid it cannot expand. When a baby scorpion starts to grow, it gets bigger, but the exoskeleton stays the same size. When it can no longer contain the growing baby, it splits open like a pair of tight pants. This is called molting.

Luckily, a new exoskeleton had formed while the scorpion was still inside the old one. But a scorpion has to be very alert just after molting. Should a predator find a scorpion before its new exoskeleton has had a few days to harden, the scorpion will be easy prey. Every time a scorpion gets bigger, it has to molt. Depending on the species, scorpions molt five or six times over a period of two to six years before reaching adulthood.

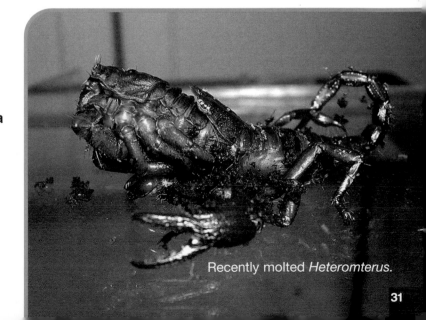

Recently molted *Heteromterus*.

Gentle Giants

Male and female emperor scorpions can grow to 8 in. (20 cm) in length. With their huge pincers, they look like little weight lifters. Male and female emperor scorpions work together to catch and chew up lizards, frogs, mice, and other small mammals to make baby food for their young, which live with their parents for two years.

Iomachus politus

It is because emperor scorpions are so gentle that they are the preferred species for people who keep scorpions as pets. They're also clean, can live up to eight years or more, and don't eat much. So if a pet that looks like a miniature Darth Vader is your thing, then an emperor scorpion just might make the perfect pet for you!

Most scorpions are solitary creatures. To socialize would be dangerous, given their habit of having relatives for dinner! Emperor scorpions are the exception. They make their homes on the floor of damp, tropical rainforests, where they live together in colonies.

Armed and Dangerous

The bulblike end of the scorpion's tail holds the glands that produce the venom. A scorpion grasps its prey in its pincers and throws its tail over its head. Then it plunges its stinger into its victim's body. The prey freezes as if hit by the rays of a tiny stun gun!

Hadrurus arizonensis

Parabuthus granulatus, Southern Africa's most venemous scorpion

Most people feel more threatened by the big variety of scorpion than the smaller kinds. That would be a mistake. Scientists who study scorpions have observed that the larger the pincers, the weaker the venom and vice versa. So, a scorpion that cannot depend on its small pincers to defend itself must rely on something else—like the strength of its venom.

The black South African fat-tailed scorpion is a small scorpion with a tail like a squirt gun that can spray venom as far as 24 in. (60 cm). Though not strong enough to kill a human, the venom is extremely painful. Should it get into a person's eye, it can cause blindness.

Parabuthus transvaalicus

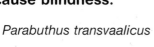

Small and Deadly!

More people die from the sting of a yellow fat-tailed scorpion than from any other. It can sting so fast that its victim doesn't know what's happening. This scorpion lives in Tunisia, Egypt, and some Middle Eastern countries. Its scientific name is *Androctonus australis*—or "southern man-killer."

Arizona is home to three species of scorpion: the giant desert hairy scorpion, the devil's scorpion, and the Arizona bark scorpion. Only one of them is dangerous. Its weak, slender pincers are the only clue that the Arizona bark scorpion's stinger is chock-full of deadly venom. Found in Arizona, southeastern California, and Utah, this is one little critter to avoid.

Centruroides exilacauda

The Brazilian *Tityus serrulatus* yellow scorpion may be just 2 in. (5 cm) long, but it is one of the most dangerous scorpions in the world. They are found in the grasslands of South America, where they hide in termites' nests. As their habitats are being destroyed, however, more and more Brazilian yellow scorpions are making their way into cities. The most amazing thing about this species is that there are no males. The ability of a female to produce young without any male participation is called parthenogenesis.

Tityus serrulatus

Daemon variegatus

Double Agents

Some arachnids copy, or mimic, scorpions. Whipscorpions have pincers, but their long, whiplike tails lack a stinger. Instead, whipscorpions defend themselves by spraying a mist of foul-smelling fluid from the base of the tail. The strong burning sensation stops predators in their tracks.

Pseudoscorpions, or false scorpions, also bear a strong resemblance to scorpions except that they have no tails or stingers. They are extremely small, with the largest measuring less than $\frac{1}{2}$ in. (1 cm) long. Their pincers have venom glands, but the venom is harmless to all but their tiny prey.

Pseudoscorpione

Despite its name, the windscorpion looks more like a spider than a scorpion. Though it has no tail, stinger, or pincers, the windscorpion does have huge jaws. With them, a wind scorpion can take down rodents, lizards, snakes, and small birds. Taking up a full third of their body, the jaws work like a combination nutcracker and knife. Ounce for ounce, these fierce arachnids deliver one of the most powerful bites of any animal.

Prey for a Cure

The venom used by scorpions to paralyze their prey may also have the power to heal. Researchers are testing venom extracted from the deathstalker scorpion in the hope it can cure certain types of brain tumors. The venom kills malignant cancer cells, while leaving healthy ones alone.

Leiurus quinquestriatus

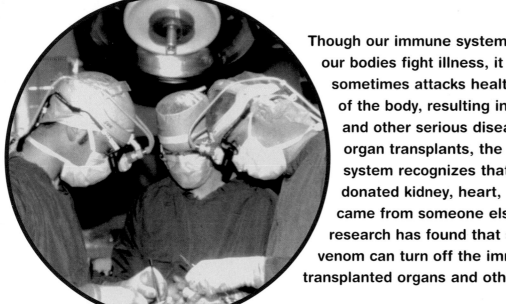

Though our immune system helps our bodies fight illness, it sometimes attacks healthy parts of the body, resulting in arthritis and other serious diseases. In organ transplants, the immune system recognizes that the donated kidney, heart, or lung came from someone else and attacks it. Recent research has found that some parts of scorpion venom can turn off the immune system, preserving transplanted organs and other healthy tissue.

Malaria, a serious disease spread by mosquitoes, has plagued millions of people who live in the tropics. Now researchers think they might have a cure. A toxin from scorpion venom has prevented malaria parasites from growing in fruit flies. If the same thing can be done with mosquitoes, it won't be long before the sting of a scorpion can wipe out this nasty disease once and for all.

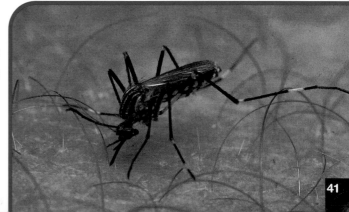

BUG, APPÉTIT!

Many people In Thailand and other Asian countries believe that eating scorpions readily available in any outdoor market can warm you up in cold weather and will even cure certain diseases. With scorpions to munch on, who needs potato chips?

Deep fried scorpions at Typhoon, a restaurant in Santa Monica, California.

Scorpion dishes are popular items on Asian restaurant menus. To ensure a steady supply, in northern Thailand, there are special scorpion farms devoted just to raising these tasty arachnids. Those that don't end up in Thai restaurants are shipped around the world so they can be enjoyed by people of other cultures.

According to David Gordon, an expert in cooking with bugs, scorpions should always be frozen before they are handled. Once they are frozen, the last segment of the tail—the one containing the venom glands, should be lopped off and thrown into the garbage. You can actually order scorpions over the Internet—hot and spicy in a can! Bon appétit!

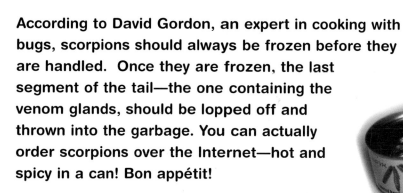

GLOSSARY

abdomen: the rear section of an arachnid, which contains its digestive, breathing, and reproductive systems, and may sometimes be segmented

arachnid: a class of animals with eight legs, two body parts, and no antennae or wings

arthropod: a group of animals with jointed legs, an exoskeleton, and no backbone

cephalothorax: the fused head and chest of an arachnid

chelicerae: an arachnid's jaws

exoskeleton: the hard outer covering that protects and supports an arachnid's body

fluoresce: to glow under a certain kind of light

fossil: a fragment, imprint, or trace of a creature or plant from the distant past

invertebrate: a creature without a backbone

molt: to shed an outgrown exoskeleton

neurotoxin: a poison that affects the nervous system

obligate: necessary for survival

parthenogenesis: the ability of a female to reproduce without a male

pectines: a pair of comblike sense organs attached to the bottom front abdomen of a scorpion

pedipalps: a scorpion's pincers

pheromones: chemical scents produced by animals

scorplings: baby scorpions

species: a group of animals with a common name that can mate and produce young

spiracles: an arthropod's breathing holes

telson: the last segment of an arthropod's body; a scorpion's telson contains its stinger

ultraviolet light: a type of light with shorter wavelengths than visible light

HADRURUS ARIZONENSIS

IOMACHUS POLITUS

ANDROCTONUS AUSTRALIS

LEIURUS QUINQUESTRIATUS

Tanzanian Long-Claw Scorpion

Common Name: Tanzanian Long-Claw Scorpion

Range: Africa

Habitat: tropical mountainous forests or grasslands

Venom: harmless

Fun Fact: Because these scorpions are not aggressive and do not sting when provoked, they are often kept as pets.

Photo credit: © Jan Ove Rein

Giant Hairy Scorpion

Common Name: Giant Hairy Scorpion

Range: Mexico and southwestern United States

Habitat: semi-arid and arid habitats

Venom: mild

Fun Fact: This is the largest scorpion found in North America.

Photo credit: © Digital Visions — Little Creatures

Death Stalker

Common Name: Death Stalker

Range: Africa and Asia

Habitat: dry habitats and desert areas

Venom: very potent

Fun Fact: As its name implies, this is a dangerous scorpion. It hides in burrows or under stones.

Photo credit: © Wolfgang Wuster

Fat Tailed Scorpion

Common Name: Fat Tailed Scorpion

Range: Africa and Asia

Habitat: dry habitats and desert areas

Venom: very potent

Fun Fact: One of the world's most dangerous scorpions, it is often found in cracks of stone and brick walls.

Photo credit: © Eric Ythier

HADOGENES TROGLODYTES

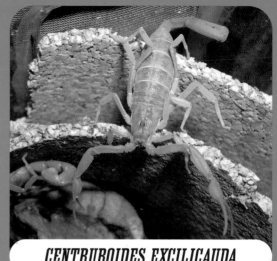

CENTRUROIDES EXCILICAUDA

PARABUTHUS GRANULATUS

SCORPIO MAURUS

🦂 Common Name: Arizona Bark Scorpion

🦂 Range: Southwestern United States and northwestern Mexico

🦂 Habitat: temperate and arid areas

🦂 Venom: potent

🦂 Fun Fact: This species comes in many different colors.

🦂 Common Name: South African Rock Scorpion

🦂 Range: Africa

🦂 Habitat: dry habitats

🦂 Venom: mild

🦂 Fun Fact: This scorpion rarely stings. Instead, it defends itself with its powerful claws.

🦂 Common Name: Israeli Gold Scorpion

🦂 Range: Africa and Asia

🦂 Habitat: dry forests and deserts

🦂 Venom: mild

🦂 Fun Fact: This was the first scorpion species to be scientifically described.

🦂 Common Name: Granulated Thick-tailed Scorpion

🦂 Range: Africa

🦂 Habitat: dry habitats

🦂 Venom: very potent

🦂 Fun Fact: Although it is one of the most venomous scorpions found in South Africa, this species can not squirt venom.